STECK-VAUGHN

Great Adventures

Henry Billings

Melissa Stone

STECK-VAUGHN
C O M P A N Y
A subsidiary of National Education Corporation

Books in this series:

Great Adventures
Great Challenges
Great Firsts
Great Heroes

Acknowledgments

Supervising Editor
Diane Sharpe

Project Editor
Teresa Turner

Designer
Sharon Golden

Electronic Production
Alan Klemp

Photo Editor
Margie Matejcik

Illustration Credits
Gary McElhaney Pp. 2-3, 5, 6; 16, 19-21, 58, 59, 60-61
Larry Raymond Pp. 38, 39, 40; 72-73, 75, 77

Cover Illustration:
Peter Angelo

Photo Credits
Pp. 10, Historical Pictures Service, Chicago; p. 12 The Granger Collection; pp. 13, 15, 26, Culver Pictures; p. 27, Historical Pictures Service, Chicago; p. 28 The Bettmann Archive; p. 29 Culver Pictures; p. 32 The Bettmann Archive; p. 33 Culver Pictures; p. 35 Historical Pictures Service, Chicago; pp. 44, 45, 47, 50, 53, 54 © Topham/The Image Works; p. 64 UPI/Bettmann Newsphotos; p. 67, 69 Culver Pictures; pp. 80, 81, 82, 83 Arlene Blum © 1979 The National Geographic Society

ISBN 0-8114-4688-3

Contents

Marco Polo

Marco Polo **squinted** in the bright desert sun. He saw only sand in all directions. Still, he felt nervous. His fellow travelers told him that the **bandit** Nogodar often rode through this area.

"Does Nogodar really have ten thousand horsemen?" Marco asked.

"Oh, yes," a friend answered. "And if he captures you, he will surely kill you or sell you as a slave."

Just then another rider stopped his horse. "Look!" he shouted. He pointed to a dark cloud of dust in the distance. "It's Nogodar! He's coming this way!"

A Narrow Escape

Most of the riders turned and galloped away. Marco was about to do the same. But suddenly his father, Nicolò Polo, called out to him.

"Marco! Stop! You will never outrun Nogodar."

"But Father," cried Marco, "what shall we do?"

"Just follow me," said Nicolò, "and you will be safe."

Silently, Marco obeyed. He knew his father was very wise. Nicolò and his brother Maffeo had spent 15 years traveling through Asia. Now, in 1271, they were making a second trip. This time they were taking 17-year-old Marco with them. Marco was delighted to be going. He wanted to share the adventures of Nicolò and Maffeo.

Nicolò told Marco to ride very slowly. "Do not kick up any dust," he warned. "It is the dust from galloping horses that Nogodar sees. If we make no dust, perhaps he will not notice us."

For hours the Polos crept eastward. At last they reached a valley. In it was a small city.

"Nogodar will not bother us here," said Nicolò.

Marco was happy to hear this. He later found out that Nogodar captured the men who galloped off. Some were sold as slaves. The rest were put to death.

In the Court of the Khan

The Polos' journey across Asia took another three years to complete. At last, in 1274, they reached China. China in those days was known as Cathay. Its leader was called a khan. In 1274, the khan was a great and powerful man named Kublai. Kublai Khan remembered Nicolò and Maffeo from their earlier trip. He welcomed them warmly.

"And who is this young man?" he asked.

"**Sire**, it is my own son to honor you," said Nicolò.

"Welcome is he, too," said the khan.

At Kublai Khan's palace, Marco saw things which amazed him. The khan was very rich. He had huge amounts of gold, jewels, and silks. Marco had never seen so many beautiful things.

Marco was also amazed by life in Cathay. The people used tools that he had never seen before. They had printing presses for books. They had coal for heating water. They used paper money. Back in Europe, people had none of these things. In almost every way, Cathay was more **advanced** than Europe. The **engineers** built better bridges. The police kept better order. The weavers made more beautiful cloth.

For the next 17 years, Marco stayed with Kublai Khan. His father and uncle also stayed. The Polos became trusted friends of the khan. Often, Kublai Khan sent Marco on special trips. Marco went to different parts of Asia and brought reports back to the khan.

Marco saw lands that no European had ever seen before. He found many strange and wonderful things. He took notes on these things. In Southern Cathay he reported seeing huge **serpents**.

"They are ten **paces** in length," he wrote. "They have two short legs, having three claws like those of a tiger. The jaws are wide enough to swallow a man, and the teeth are large and sharp. Their whole appearance is so frightening that neither man, nor any kind of animal, can approach them without terror."

To Marco, these creatures seemed **fantastic**. Today they do not seem so wild. We call them crocodiles.

Return to Italy

Although the Polos were happy in Cathay, they missed Italy. They longed to return to their hometown of Venice. One day Marco told the khan that the Polos wished to leave Cathay. Kublai Khan became upset.

"You cannot go!" he said. "I could not bear to lose such good friends and **advisers**. You must never speak of it again!"

The Polos did not know what to do. They did not dare go against the orders of the khan. Sadly, they decided they would have to stay in Cathay forever. In 1291, however, they finally had a chance to leave. Princess Kukachin of Cathay was asked to marry the king of Persia. Men came from Persia to take the girl on the long and dangerous journey.

"There are many bandits and unfriendly tribes along the way," Kublai Khan said to Marco. "How can I be sure Princess Kukachin arrives in Persia safely?"

"Why not have her travel by sea?" suggested Marco.

"That would be safer," answered Kublai, "but the Persians do not know how to sail a ship."

"I could go with them. I have sailed the Indian Ocean several times in my travels for you," said Marco.

The khan liked this idea. He agreed to let Marco, Nicolò, and Maffeo sail with the princess to Persia. In return for this favor, Kublai Khan told the Polos they could return to Italy.

The trip to Persia was long and difficult. It took two years to complete. From Persia, the Polos continued on to Europe. In 1295, they finally arrived in Italy.

In 1298, Marco wrote a book about his travels. He called it The Travels of Marco Polo. Few people believed what he wrote. They thought he was making up wild lies. It was only after his death that Europeans began to believe him. In the 1400's, one reader who believed him was Christopher Columbus. It was Polo's book that **inspired** Columbus to make his great journey.

Do You Remember?

■ In the blank, write the letter of the best ending for each sentence.

_____ 1. Nogodar was a
   a. king.   b. weaver.   c. bandit.

_____ 2. The leader of China was called
   a. Cathay.   b. a khan.   c. Maffeo.

_____ 3. In the 1200's, people in Europe had no
   a. horses.   b. paper money.   c. ships.

_____ 4. Marco traveled to different parts of
   a. Asia.   b. Canada.   c. Africa.

_____ 5. Marco helped Princess Kukachin get to
   a. Europe.   b. America.   c. Persia.

Critical Thinking – Fact or Opinion?

■ A **fact** can be proven. An **opinion** is a belief. Opinions cannot be proven. Write **F** before each statement that is a fact. Write **O** before each statement that is an opinion.

_____ 1. Marco Polo was smarter than Kublai Khan.

_____ 2. Nogodar was a bandit.

_____ 3. Kublai Khan owned many jewels.

_____ 4. Crocodiles are ugly animals.

_____ 5. Marco saw lands that no European had seen before.

_____ 6. Kublai Khan was a selfish man.

_____ 7. Marco Polo sailed across the Indian Ocean several times.

_____ 8. In 1291, Princess Kukachin left Cathay.

_____ 9. It was foolish of Marco to leave Cathay.

_____ 10. Christopher Columbus believed what Marco Polo wrote.

Exploring Words

■ Write the correct word in each sentence.

Sire	engineers	fantastic	advisers	bandit
serpents	advanced	inspired	squinted	paces

1. Something that is very strange is _____.

2. You can use _____ to measure the length of something.

3. A king is called _____.

4. A person who robs and steals is a _____.

5. To be ahead of others is to be _____.

6. People who make plans for building things are _____.

7. Snakes and snake-like animals are _____.

8. If something _____ you, it made you want to do something.

9. People who help you decide what to do are _____.

10. If you looked at something with your eyes partly closed, you

_____

Amazing Voyage

Captain William Bligh lay asleep in his cabin on the H.M.S. Bounty. It was just before dawn on April 28, 1789. Suddenly the door to Bligh's cabin swung open. Fletcher Christian, a crew member, stood in the doorway. Christian grabbed the captain and pulled him out of bed.

"What are you doing?" cried Bligh.

"I'm taking control of the ship," snarled Christian. "Don't make another sound, or I'll kill you right now."

Set Adrift

Captain Bligh couldn't believe what was happening. It was against the law for a crew member to take control of a ship. Such action was called a **mutiny**. Death by hanging was **punishment** for this. Christian knew this, but he didn't care. He hated Captain Bligh.

Christian dragged Bligh out of his cabin. Several other men helped him. Together, they forced Bligh off the main ship and into a small, open boat. Eighteen of the crew members refused to join the mutiny. They were thrown into the boat with Bligh.

Slowly the Bounty sailed away from the small boat. Bligh and the others watched it go. As they did, their minds filled with fear. It seemed certain they would die. They were in the middle of the Pacific Ocean. The nearest friendly island, Timor, was 3,800 miles away. Their boat gave them no shelter from sun or storms. It contained only five days' worth of food and water.

For a few minutes, Captain Bligh felt fear rising inside him. But then he took a deep breath. He could see that his men depended on him. They were staring at him with large, frightened eyes.

"I won't let these men down," he thought. "I'll do my best to lead them to safety."

Captain Bligh

A Long and Painful Trip

Bligh turned the sail of the boat to the west. He told the men they were going to sail all the way to Timor.

"It's a long trip over little-known waters," he warned. "In order to make it, we'll have to **ration** the food. Every man will get an **ounce** of bread and a half cup of water each day. That way the food will last three or four weeks."

The men all promised not to eat more than their share. They also agreed to take turns steering the boat.

For the first four days, the weather was clear. The boat moved smoothly through the water. On the fifth day, however, the weather turned bad. Wind and rain tore at the sail. Waves crashed over the boat and filled it with water. Bligh **struggled** to keep the boat from tipping over. His men **bailed** water out of the boat. Hour after hour they worked. The storm lasted all day and all night. It even continued the next day.

After two days, the storm finally died down. By then the men were **exhausted**. They were wet and cold and hungry. The bread on the boat was wet. Most of it had started to **rot**.

The men tried to stretch out and go to sleep. But there was not much room in the boat. They lay crowded on the floor of the boat. The next day, a new storm blew in. This one lasted thirteen days. It seemed that the rain, wind, and lightning would never end.

Bligh could see that his men were losing hope. Their bones ached and their muscles **cramped**. Many had terrible pain in their stomachs. Everyone was weak and growing weaker. Some were half dead already.

Bligh still hoped the men would make it to Timor. But he saw that it might take longer than he had planned. New storms might slow them down or drive them off course. Then they would run out of food before they reached Timor. Bligh decided to cut the men's rations in half. It seemed cruel. But it was the only way to make the food last.

Sun Through The Clouds

By May 25, all the men were near death. Bligh worried that one more cold, stormy night would finish them off. Luckily, that night the rain stopped. The wind died down. Waves no longer crashed over the boat.

The next day, the sun broke through the clouds. Bligh felt a small burst of hope. Later that day, something wonderful happened. The men saw birds flying overhead. Surely this meant that land was nearby. At once the men became more cheerful. When a bird landed on the edge of the boat, they grabbed it with their bare hands. This small amount of meat lifted everyone's spirits. It gave them the strength to stay alive. The next day the men caught another bird. It, too, gave the men new hope.

On May 28, the men spotted land. Bligh warned them not to get too excited. He had been keeping careful notes on how far the boat had sailed. He knew that Timor was still far away.

"We can stop and look for food," he said. "But then we must move on. We must reach Timor before all our strength is gone."

Captain Bligh and his men arrive on Timor.

Along the shore the men gathered coconuts and **clams**. But soon, an angry tribe appeared and drove them back out to sea.

As they sailed west, they hit rough waters. Again and again water splashed into their boat. At night they shivered with cold. In the daytime, the sun brought new problems. The men became sick from the heat. Their skin burned and peeled. Many also had awful cramps in their stomachs.

At last, after 41 days, Bligh and his men saw Timor in the distance. Tears of joy ran down their faces. When they reached the island, they crawled off the boat and fell onto the sandy shore. They were all half-starved. Their clothes were rotten, and their bodies were covered with sores. Still, they were alive. Thanks to Captain Bligh, they had lived through one of the most amazing voyages ever.

Do You Remember?

■ Read each sentence below. Write **T** if the sentence is true. Write **F** if the sentence is false.

_____ 1. Fletcher Christian was captain of the H.M.S. Bounty.

_____ 2. All of the crew members joined in the mutiny.

_____ 3. Bligh rationed the food.

_____ 4. Three of Bligh's men died during a storm.

_____ 5. Birds were a sign that land was nearby.

_____ 6. Bligh's toes and fingers froze.

_____ 7. The men stopped at one island and gathered coconuts and clams.

_____ 8. It took 41 days for Bligh and his men to reach Timor.

Express Yourself

■ Pretend that you are one of Bligh's men. Write a letter to a friend back home explaining why you refused to join the mutiny.

Dear _____

_____

_____

_____

_____

_____

_____

16

Exploring Words

■ Read each sentence. Fill in the circle next to the best meaning for the word in dark print. If you need help, use the Glossary.

1. Fletcher Christian led the **mutiny**.
   - ○ a. group of musicians
   - ○ b. a dance
   - ○ c. sailors rising up against the captain

2. Christian knew the **punishment** for mutiny.
   - ○ a. name
   - ○ b. something done to someone who has broken a rule
   - ○ c. right way to do it

3. Captain Bligh had to **ration** the food.
   - ○ a. cook well   ○ b. give out in equal shares   ○ c. throw out

4. Each man got one **ounce** of bread.
   - ○ a. a measure of weight   ○ b. bite   ○ c. loaf

5. The men **struggled** during storms.
   - ○ a. argued   ○ b. worked very hard   ○ c. got lost

6. The men **bailed** water for hours without stopping.
   - ○ a. drank   ○ b. heated   ○ c. emptied out

7. When they reached Timor, the men were **exhausted**.
   - ○ a. very tired   ○ b. angry   ○ c. happy

8. The food on the ship began to **rot**.
   - ○ a. go bad   ○ b. grow roots   ○ c. roll

9. As the men sat in the boat, their muscles **cramped**.
   - ○ a. became painfully tight   ○ b. grew   ○ c. stretched

10. They gathered **clams** before returning to the boat.
    - ○ a. nuts   ○ b. shellfish   ○ c. money

Search for the Niger

Mungo Park looked at the map spread out before him. It was a map of Africa. Parts of the map were **blank**. There were many places in Africa that Europeans still had not explored.

"I'd love to be the man who discovers which way the Niger River flows," said Park to a friend.

The friend laughed. "No one will ever learn that. The river is impossible to follow. It's surrounded by rain forests, deserts, and unfriendly people."

"I know," said Park. "Still, I'd like to try."

Heading Off Alone

Park was not the only one who wondered about the Niger. Many people in Great Britain wanted to discover its secrets. "Does it flow west or east?" they asked themselves. "Is it part of the Nile River or Congo River or neither?"

In 1794, a group of men in Great Britain decided to find out. They offered to pay someone to explore the Niger. Mungo Park quickly **volunteered** for the job. He knew it would be dangerous. Two earlier explorers had tried to find the Niger. Both had died before reaching the river. Still, 23-year-old Park was not frightened. He was eager for adventure.

Park was supposed to take 50 men with him on his search for the Niger. But he got tired of waiting for volunteers. Finally he said to himself, "I'll go now, and I'll go alone."

Park reached the coast of West Africa in July 1795. Right away he came down with a fever. For several months he was ill. By December he felt better.

On December 2, 1795, he set off on his search for the Niger.

Held Captive

Park took a guide and a servant with him. He also took a horse and two donkeys. In his pack he carried a **compass** and four guns. Park rode through many African countries. Then he crossed into lands where the people were **Moslems**. These people hated Christians. Park wrote in his **diary**, "Everywhere I went they hissed, shouted, and even **spat** in my face."

In the country of Ludamar, a band of horsemen captured Park. They dragged him to Ali, the king of Ludamar. Ali kept Park a prisoner for four months. Finally, Ali's messengers announced that they would kill him. But first they said they would cut off his right hand. Then they would put his eyes out.

Luckily, Ali did not have a chance to carry out these actions. On the night of July 1, while his guards slept, Park escaped. He took nothing with him but his compass and a horse.

Reaching the Niger

Park was safe from Ali. But he was in the desert without water. He was certain he would die. But a sudden shower saved him. He spread out his clothes to catch the rain. Then he drank the rainwater by **sucking** on the wet clothes.

At last Park joined a friendly group from the Bambara tribe. They took him to the town of Ségou. It was here, on July 20, 1796, that he first saw the Niger. He wrote, "I saw with pleasure the great object of my **mission**–the **majestic** Niger."

As Park began following the river, he grew weak. The sun beat down on him. Mosquitos covered him with bites. He had no food and no medicine.

On July 29, both Park and his horse **collapsed**. Park was in bad shape. He had no money. He was worn out from being sick and hungry. With his horse gone, he would have to walk. The rain poured down on him. With a sinking heart, Park decided to turn back.

But could he get back? He began to walk across flooded fields. His body shook from fever. Word spread that he was a spy for the Bambara. Villages closed their gates to him. At times people even chased him with sticks as if he were a stray dog.

One day, a group of men with guns surrounded him. These men forced Park to hand over his compass and some of his clothes. Then they disappeared, leaving him alone. Park felt worse than he ever had in his life. He prepared himself to die. He dropped his head and stared at the ground. There he noticed a tiny flower. He thought, "How could a God who created such a beautiful plant in such a lonely spot forget about me?"

Suddenly Park felt that his God had not forgotten him. He was filled with new hope. He decided not to

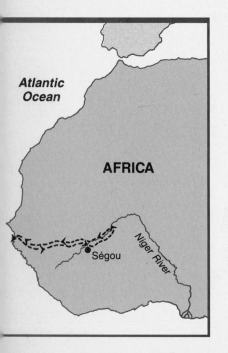

quit. Somehow he dragged himself to the next town.
This time the people opened the gates. They were kind
to him. Slowly his fever died down, and his strength
returned. He made his way back to the West African
coast. On April 19, 1797, Mungo Park headed back to
Great Britain.

In April 1805, Park returned to Africa. He wanted to
try again to discover the path of the Niger. This time he
brought 40 men with him. During the long journey to
the river, however, most of these men died. When the
group reached the Niger on August 19, only Park and
ten others were still alive. By November the number
had dropped to five.

That same month, Park sent a letter home to Great
Britain. In it he wrote, "Though all Europeans who are
with me should die, and though I were myself half dead,
I would still go on; and if I could not succeed in the
object of my journey, I would at least die on the Niger."
These were the last words heard from Mungo Park. On
November 20, 1805, Park and his men set off down the
Niger in a canoe. They were never seen again.

Do You Remember?

■ In the blank, write the letter of the best ending for each sentence.

_____ 1. Park was paid by men from
    a. West Africa. b. Great Britain. c. the United States.

_____ 2. The king of Ludamar, Ali, planned to
    a. teach Park. b. trade with Park. c. kill Park.

_____ 3. Members of the Bambara tribe took Park to
    a. Ali. b. the Niger. c. the Congo.

_____ 4. Park felt new hope when he noticed a
    a. rainbow. b. tiny flower. c. beautiful sunrise.

_____ 5. After Mungo and his men set off down the Niger in a canoe in 1805, they
    a. were never seen again.
    b. decided to turn back.
    c. returned to England.

Critical Thinking — Drawing Conclusions

■ Finish each sentence by writing the best answer.

1. Park offered to search for the Niger because _____

_____

2. Park ran away from Ali because _____

_____

3. On his first trip, Park stopped following the Niger because _____

_____

4. On his first trip, Park set out to search for the Niger alone because

_____

_____

Exploring Words

■ Use the words in the box to complete the paragraphs. Reread the paragraphs to be sure they make sense.

| mission | sucking | volunteered | compass | collapsed |
| spat | majestic | blank | Moslems | diary |

In 1794, Park **(1)** _____ to explore the Niger. This part of Africa was **(2)** _____ on European maps. Park took only a few things with him. He took a gun and a **(3)** _____ . He also took a **(4)** _____ to write down what he learned.

Park's **(5)** _____ proved to be very difficult. He suffered a great deal. Unfriendly **(6)** _____ bothered him. They **(7)** _____ in his face. One group even kept him prisoner for several months. In the desert he grew very thirsty. He got water by **(8)** _____ his clothes after a rain storm. At last Park did reach the Niger. It was a **(9)** _____ river. But by this time he and his horse were both growing weaker. On July 29, they **(10)** _____. Park was forced to turn around and head back to West Africa.

Henry Morton Stanley

Henry Morton Stanley stood on the bank of the Lualaba River.

"At last I have reached it," he whispered. For two years Stanley and his helpers had been searching for this river. They had wandered through 6,000 miles of Central African jungles. They had suffered from **disease** and hunger. They had faced many **hostile** Africans. But now, at last, they had found the river. "Now," said Stanley, "the real work can begin."

The Long Search

Stanley's plan was to follow the Lualaba River to its end. Did it flow north into the Nile? Or did it turn west and become the Congo? No European knew the answer. The European map of Central Africa just showed a blank space.

Stanley set out in November 1874. He took 356 workers with him. Most were Africans from Zanzibar. These workers carried food and other supplies. Day after day they cut their way through thick jungle vines. Their backs ached from carrying heavy supply bags. Their feet became **bloody** and sore. Some grew sick and died.

"We will never find the Lualaba," one worker grumbled. This man decided to leave Stanley. Others soon followed. By the time Stanley reached the Lualaba, he had lost dozens of workers.

New Troubles

Stanley planned to float down the Lualaba River. He had even brought a boat with him. His workers had been carrying the boat in pieces. Now Stanley ordered them to put the pieces together.

When the boat was ready, Stanley and a few others climbed in. The rest would have to walk along the shore. Stanley hoped to get more boats soon. He also hoped to get more food. He thought he could trade with villagers along the way. But these people were frightened of him. To them, Stanley's group looked like a hostile army. Whenever Stanley approached, the villagers attacked. Sometimes the attacks turned into bloody battles. Several times Stanley's people were lucky to escape with their lives.

"This trip is turning into a **nightmare**," Stanley thought. "Food supplies are running out. The workers are tired. Many are too sick to keep going."

Finally, Stanley let his men steal some canoes. The workers climbed in. Over 70 of them were nearly dead.

Henry Morton Stanley

Fighting the Terrible River

Each day things got worse. The water turned rough. **Rapids** tossed the canoes around like toys. Several workers drowned when their canoes tipped over.

Giant waterfalls also slowed the group. The workers had to leave the water. They carried their canoes down cliffs. Healthy workers carried sick ones. It was slow, back-breaking work. Everyone, even Stanley, was wearing out.

As the weeks passed, Stanley saw that the river was turning west. "The Lualaba is not the **source** of the Nile," he wrote. "Now I know that this terrible river will lead us to the Atlantic." Stanley was right. The Lualaba

turned into the Congo, the great river of Central Africa.

To Stanley, the Congo seemed to go on forever. There were more rapids and more waterfalls. In one short stretch, 13 men drowned, and many canoes were lost. At last, on August 9, 1877, Stanley reached the Atlantic coast. There the river emptied into the ocean.

The trip had killed most of his workers. Only 115 out of 356 were still with him. Stanley himself weighed just 96 pounds. His hair had turned completely white. Yet he wrote, "Our wars and troubles are over. We have **pierced** the dark **continent** from east to west, and **traced** its **mightiest** river to the ocean."

Do You Remember?

■ Read each sentence below. Write **T** if the sentence is true. Write **F** if the sentence is false.

_____ 1. Most of Stanley's workers were Africans from Zanzibar.

_____ 2. African villagers never attacked Stanley and his group.

_____ 3. Stanley let his men steal canoes from African villagers.

_____ 4. The Lualaba River turned into the Nile.

_____ 5. The Congo is a river in Central Africa.

_____ 6. Stanley never made it to the Atlantic coast.

_____ 7. All of Stanley's workers died during the trip.

_____ 8. At the end of his trip, Stanley weighed just 96 pounds.

Express Yourself

■ Pretend you are Henry Morton Stanley. You are in the middle of your trip through Central Africa. Many of your workers want to give up and leave you. Write down what you would say to them to convince them to keep going.

_____

_____

_____

_____

_____

_____

Exploring Words

■ Use the clues to complete the puzzle. Choose from the words in the box.

disease

hostile

bloody

nightmare

rapids

source

pierced

continent

mightiest

traced

Across

2. covered with blood
5. largest or strongest
7. a large piece of land
8. part of a river where water flows very fast
10. sickness

Down

1. unfriendly
3. went all the way through
4. bad dream
6. followed the course of
9. the place something comes from

Around the World

Nellie Bly ran up to her **editor's** office in New York City. Jules Chambers, editor of the newspaper the World, had a new **assignment** for her. "How would you like to travel around the world?" he asked.

Nellie smiled. "I'd love to!"

"You'd be in a race," Chambers warned.

"What kind of race?" Nellie asked.

"A race against time."

"Against Phineas Fogg's time?"

"Oh, you couldn't possibly beat that."

"Yes, I could," said Nellie. "Just watch me."

Nellie Bly sails for Great Britain.

A Bold Promise

In 1872, Jules Verne wrote a story called Around the World in 80 Days. Its hero was Phineas Fogg. Fogg won a bet by circling the world in just 80 days. At the time that seemed impossible. But now, in 1889, Nellie Bly wanted to beat Fogg's **imaginary** record.

Chambers thought it would make a great story. But he didn't really think Nellie could do it. Travel in those days was difficult. The trains were slow and often late. No one knew for sure when a ship might sail.

But Nellie was a tough newspaper **reporter**. She was willing to do anything to get a story. "I'll make it back to New York in just seventy-five days!" she told Chambers.

She's Off

On November 14, 1889, Nellie sailed for Great Britain. She had never been to sea before. The ship rocked wildly in the rough waves. Nellie got **seasick** during the first day. One man laughed at her. He said, "You'll never make it around the world!"

But Nellie quickly got used to sailing. By the second day she felt wonderful. Some of the others were not so lucky. A huge wave washed two sailors **overboard**. Many passengers got very ill. Even the man who laughed at Nellie became seasick. Finally, after six stormy days, the ship landed in England.

Back in New York, Chambers kept readers **informed** about Nellie's adventure. He put a map of her route on the front page of the World. Fan mail poured in to the newspaper. People wrote songs about Nellie. They named racehorses after her. The newspaper **boasted**, "The whole **civilized** world is watching Nellie Bly."

Breaking the Record

Things didn't go smoothly for Nellie. She had to jump onto a moving train in London. She almost missed others. But her plans depended on getting a ship for Asia. When would one sail? In Italy she got lucky. She caught the Victoria just as it was about to sail.

In Singapore she saw a small monkey locked in a cage. Nellie's heart nearly broke at the sight. She decided to buy the animal. From then on, the monkey went wherever she went.

On January 7, 1890, Nellie left Japan on board the Oceanic. Three days out the weather turned bad. Strong winds and high waves battered the ship. The Oceanic didn't get very far. Some sailors blamed Nellie's monkey.

"Your monkey is bringing us bad luck," they said. "You've got to get rid of it! Throw it overboard!"

Nellie refused. She prayed the storm would end. Then she could still make it to New York on time. But with each passing day, she grew more worried. Time was running out.

THE WORLD

GUARANTEED GREATER THAN THAT OF ANY TWO OTHER AMERICAN NEWSPAPERS COMBINED.

CIRCULATION BOOKS OPEN TO ALL.

CIRCULATION PER DAY DURING THE MONTH OF DECEMBER, 1889, -- 340,113 COPIES

E FIVE CENTS.

NEW YORK, SUNDAY, JANUARY 26, 1890.

PRICE FIVE

SHE'S BROKEN EVERY RECORD!

A Little Pardonable Consternation Among the Globe-Circlers at the Remarkable Achievement of "The World's" Traveller.

Verne Followed Every Step of the Journey on His Globes.

THE WORLD correspondent then asked:

FATHER TIME OUTDONE !

ALL EUROPE ENTHUSIASTIC.

Congratulations from Geographers, Scientists and Friends.

VERN

Even

the

HER T

Thous

WELCOME

The W

NELL

"I can't go back to New York a **failure**," she thought. "I would rather die than fail."

At last the weather improved, and the ship made it to San Francisco. Nellie and her monkey quickly hopped onto the first train headed for New York. On January 25, she crossed the finish line.

"She's done it!" officials announced. "She's broken Phineas Fogg's record!" Nellie Bly had circled the world in seventy-two days, six hours, ten minutes and eleven seconds!

Do You Remember?

■ Read each sentence below. Write **T** if the sentence is true. Write **F** if the sentence is false.

_____ 1. Phineas Fogg was a real person.

_____ 2. Nellie Bly was a reporter for the World.

_____ 3. Nellie was washed overboard on her way to England.

_____ 4. Nellie sailed from Italy to Asia on the Victoria.

_____ 5. In Singapore, Nellie bought a puppy.

_____ 6. Sailors wanted Nellie to throw her monkey overboard.

_____ 7. Nellie Bly beat Phineas Fogg's record.

_____ 8. Jules Verne married Nellie Bly.

Critical Thinking – Fact or Opinion?

■ Write **F** before each statement that is a fact. Write **O** before each statement that is an opinion.

_____ 1. Everyone should read Around the World in 80 Days.

_____ 2. Nellie sailed on the Oceanic from Japan to San Francisco.

_____ 3. It was foolish of Nellie to buy a monkey.

_____ 4. Nellie got seasick on the way to England.

_____ 5. Nellie Bly crossed the finish line on January 25, 1890.

_____ 6. Jules Chambers should have gone with Nellie.

_____ 7. Some people wrote songs about Nellie Bly.

_____ 8. Nellie Bly was braver than Mungo Park.

36

Exploring Words

■ Use the words in the box to complete the paragraphs. Reread the paragraphs to be sure they make sense.

boasted	assignment	failure	editor	reporter
civilized	overboard	imaginary	seasick	informed

Nellie Bly was a **(1)** _____ for the <u>World</u>. Her

(2) _____ was Jules Chambers. In 1889, Chambers gave Nellie

an exciting **(3)** _____. He asked her to travel around the world

as quickly as possible. Nellie **(4)** _____ that she could make

the trip in 75 days. That would beat Phineas Fogg's

(5) _____ record.

Nellie ran into many problems during her travels. The trip to England

was very rough. Nellie and the other passengers became

(6) _____. Two men were even washed **(7)** _____.

Meanwhile, back in New York, Chambers kept readers **(8)** _____

about Nellie's trip. He said that everyone in the **(9)** _____ world

was watching her. Nellie worried that she would not make it back in

time. Then she would feel like a **(10)** _____. Luckily, she was

able to get back to New York in just 72 days.

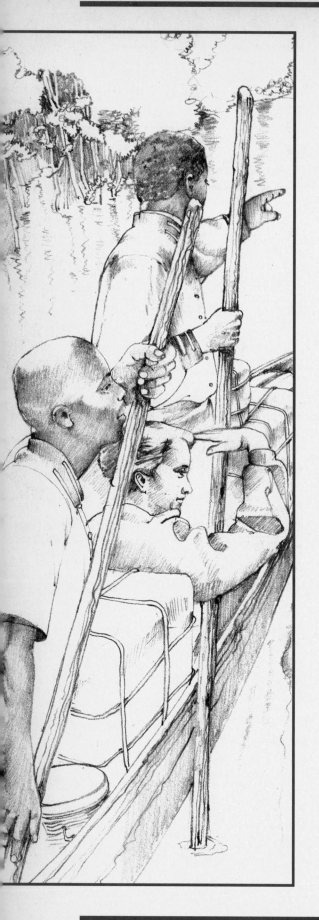

Mary Kingsley

Mary Kingsley sat in a canoe in the middle of the Karkola River. Sounds of birds and wild animals floated through the air. Mary was excited. She was the first European to travel into this part of the West African jungle. As she paddled along, one of her African guides pointed to a cliff.

"There is M'fetta, a Fang village," he said.

"Are the Fang really **cannibals**?" asked Mary.

The guide nodded. "They kill their enemies and eat them."

Among the Fang

Mary entered M'fetta on July 23, 1895. She walked into the village calmly. She showed no fear. Her guides were nervous. They were afraid the Fang would kill them. Luckily, one of the Fang had traded with one of the guides before. These two men recognized each other. The chief allowed the guide to speak.

"The white woman is a trader," the guide said. "She will trade her fish hooks and colored cloth for your **ivory** and rubber."

The Fang nodded. They would trade with Mary. Mary was a good trader. She was tough, but fair. The people in M'fetta decided they could trust her. Three of the men even agreed to join her party and lead her to other Fang villages. These three men were Kiva, Fika, and Wiki.

Mary was pleased by her success. She knew her friends thought she was crazy to be in Africa. Most people didn't think a quiet English lady could **survive** in the jungles. But Mary wanted to be an explorer. She had come to Africa to collect tropical fish for the British Museum. But she had also come to learn about the people. She didn't want to judge the Africans. She wanted to understand them.

Danger Everywhere

After leaving M'fetta, Mary went deeper into Fang country. Each day she faced new dangers. **Poisonous** snakes hung from trees. Beds of quicksand lay hidden under the grass.

Mary also learned more about the Fang. Kiva and Wiki showed her how to collect rubber from rubber

trees. She heard Fang music and watched their dances. She learned how the Fang hunted and fished.

One day Mary fell into an elephant trap. Wiki saved her by throwing her a vine and pulling her out. Another day she and her guides came to a huge swamp. Hour after hour they **waded** neck-deep through the dirty water. At last they reached dry ground. By then their hands and necks were covered with **leeches**. The leeches had sucked so much of Mary's blood that she almost fainted.

Telling Her Story

In one Fang village, Mary was invited to spend the night. She noticed a small bag hanging on the wall. When Mary opened the bag, she was **shocked**. It contained human ears, toes, and eyes.

This would have frightened most people. But Mary thought of it as an **opportunity** to learn more about the Fang. Calmly she asked Wiki about the bag.

"We Fang not only eat our enemies," he told her. "We also eat dead family members. We keep bits of the bodies to help remember these people. It's our way of honoring the dead."

When Mary returned to England, she wrote a book about her travels. At that time, most Europeans wanted to change the old African ways of life. Mary believed this was wrong. In her book, Mary tried to show these people that Africans were not **savages**. She said they were part of a great world race and ought to be respected. Mary worked for the rest of her life to **convince** other Europeans to respect African ways of life.

Do You Remember?

■ In the blank, write the letter of the best ending for each sentence.

_____ 1. M'fetta was
   a. a Fang village.
   b. an English explorer.
   c. an African guide.

_____ 2. Mary traded fish hooks and colored cloth for
   a. snake skins.   b. rubber.   c. elephant traps.

_____ 3. Kiva, Fika, and Wiki were
   a. members of the Fang tribe.
   b. types of rubber trees.
   c. rivers in West Africa.

_____ 4. Mary opened a bag of
   a. leeches.
   b. human body parts.
   c. teeth from wild animals.

_____ 5. Mary tried to
   a. teach the Fang.
   b. fool the Fang.
   c. understand the Fang.

Express Yourself

■ Pretend you are a member of the Fang tribe. Mary Kingsley has just walked into your village. It is the first time you have ever seen a European. Tell what you think about this strange person.

_____

_____

_____

_____

_____

Exploring Words

■ Write the correct word in each sentence.

cannibals	ivory	survive	poisonous	waded
leeches	shocked	savages	opportunity	convince

1. To live through something is to _____.

2. Something that can kill or cause harm with poison is _____.

3. A chance to do something is an _____.

4. People who eat other humans are _____.

5. To be very surprised is to be _____.

6. Worms that drink human blood are called _____.

7. To make people believe something is to _____ them.

8. People whose way of life is rough and wild are called _____.

9. If you walked through water, you _____ through it.

10. The tusks of an elephant are _____.

Flight of the Eagle

Salomon Andrée stuck his head out the door. A blast of cold air hit his face. Once again, the wind was blowing from the wrong direction. "Doesn't this wind ever blow from the south?" he asked himself.

Andrée, a Swedish explorer, was waiting on Danes' Island with his team. He wanted to travel in a hot-air balloon over the North Pole 720 miles away. But he needed a south wind. It never came. Finally, on August 19, 1896, he gave up. Winter was coming to the North Pole. But Andrée promised, "We'll be back next year."

Andrée and his team lived and worked in the basket of the Eagle.

Getting Ready

On May 29, 1897, Andrée and his team did return to Danes' Island. They brought with them a 78-foot-high silk balloon. It was called the Eagle. The men checked all its **seams**. They gave it a special **varnish** to stop any leaks. They carefully tested each piece of **equipment**. By July 1, the Eagle was ready. Andrée hooked on a basket. It would carry him, Nils Strindberg, and Knut Fraenkel over the North Pole. The only thing missing was a south wind. So again the men sat back and waited.

On the night of July 10, Andrée said, "I feel that it will not be long before we shall go up." He was right.

The next morning a joyful cry rang out. Some of the men had gotten up early. They felt the wind blowing from the south. "Southward!" they all shouted. "A strong and steady south wind!"

Off for the North Pole

Everyone jumped out of bed. Andrée met with Fraenkel, Strindberg, and the others. "Is this the day?" he asked. The wind was a bit stronger than he liked. Still, the men agreed they should go ahead. Andrée gave the order to prepare the balloon for liftoff.

Quickly the men went to work. A quiet fear gripped them all. Would the three men make it? Would they come back alive? No one had ever flown a hot-air balloon over the North Pole.

Soon the time for worrying was over. It was time for action. Andrée jumped into the basket. Strindberg and Fraenkel followed him. At exactly 2:30 P.M., Andrée gave the order. He shouted, "Cut the ropes."

The huge balloon rose **gracefully**. The men on the ground cried out, "Good luck to Andrée!" The three men yelled back, "Salute old Sweden!"

The Fate of the Eagle

At first, all went well. The balloon headed north. It rose to 1,500 feet, and traveled about 25 miles an hour. Later that day, Andrée sent back his first message by dropping a floating marker into the sea. It read, "July 11, 10 P.M. We are now over ice. **Glorious** weather. **Excellent** spirits."

On July 13, Andrée sent back another message. This time he used a **carrier pigeon**. The message read simply, "Good journey northward."

The crew on the ground believed everything was going smoothly. But, up in the air, the three men must have been having trouble. After the 13th, no more messages arrived. Day after day the ground crew waited. But the men were never heard from again.

Search parties were sent to look for the men. They

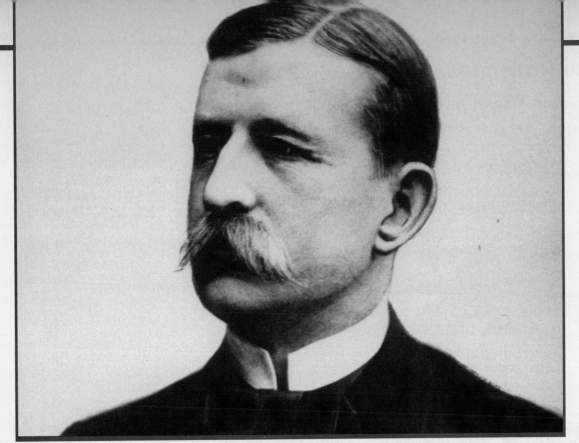

Salomon Andrée

found nothing. It seemed that their **fate** would be forever locked in the Arctic ice. Thirty-three years later, however, the mystery was solved. An explorer named Gunnar Horn went to White Island. There he stumbled across the frozen bodies of the three men.

Experts believe that something went wrong with the balloon. Andrée had to make a landing. He and his men set up camp on the ice. There Strindberg died from **illness** or accident. Later Andrée and Fraenkel were cooking a meal inside their tent. A poisonous gas called carbon monoxide came from their stove. Carbon monoxide has no **odor**. The two men had no way of knowing that the stove was leaking. They died without knowing that they were in danger.

Do You Remember?

■ Read each sentence below. Write **T** if the sentence is true. Write **F** if the sentence is false.

_____ 1. Salomon Andrée was a Swedish explorer.

_____ 2. On Danes' Island, Andrée and his men waited for a north wind.

_____ 3. The Eagle was the name of Andrée's balloon.

_____ 4. Andrée's balloon could travel 200 miles per hour.

_____ 5. Andrée dropped a floating marker into the sea.

_____ 6. Fraenkel died when he jumped out of the balloon.

_____ 7. Gunnar Horn found the bodies of Andrée, Strindberg, and Fraenkel.

_____ 8. Carbon monoxide has a terrible odor.

Critical Thinking — Main Ideas

■ Underline the two most important ideas from the story.

1. Salomon Andrée's balloon was a 78-foot-high silk balloon.

2. Salomon Andrée tried to reach the North Pole.

3. Gunnar Horn explored White Island in 1930.

4. Salomon Andrée never returned from his 1897 trip to the Arctic.

5. The deadly gas Andrée's stove leaked was called carbon monoxide.

Exploring Words

■ Use the clues to complete the puzzle. Choose from the words in the box.

excellent

carrier pigeon

odor

illness

glorious

seams

fate

varnish

equipment

gracefully

Across
1. wonderful
5. bird taught to carry messages
7. being sick
9. type of paint that forms a hard, clear surface
10. what happens to a person

Down
2. smell
3. very good
4. in a smooth and easy way
6. things that have a special use
8. places where pieces of cloth are sewn together

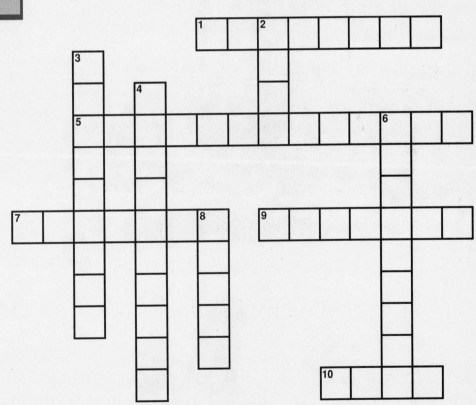

Sir Ernest Shackleton

On December 23, 1915, Sir Ernest Shackleton gave the order to march. He and his 27 men began the long journey across the frozen ocean. As they moved along, they saw no land. There were only huge **slabs** of ice in all directions.

With each step, they broke through the top **layer**. Freezing water washed around their knees. Shackleton saw the men struggling. He called one man over to him.

"We may not live through this march," he said. "Leave this note back at our camp. It explains what we are doing. Perhaps someday someone will find it. Then the world will know what happened to us."

Floating On Ice

As the group stumbled along, Sir Ernest thought about the last few months. In December 1914, he and his team had set sail for Antarctica. They had hoped to be the first people to cross the frozen continent on foot. They never reached land, however. Their ship had gotten stuck in ice. For nine months they had been trapped, surrounded by huge slabs of ice called **floes**. One man said they were like an almond in a chocolate bar. Finally the ice tore the ship apart. The group had been forced to leave it.

"And so here we are, 200 miles from the nearest island," Shackleton thought, "and 1,000 miles from the nearest humans."

After five days of marching, Sir Ernest told the men to stop. They had gone only ten miles, and the march was wearing them out.

"We will find a **solid** ice floe and pitch our tents," he announced. "Then we will wait. When the ice breaks up, we will **launch** the lifeboats."

For three months they waited. Day after day the wind whipped their faces. The temperature dipped to below zero. Food supplies ran low. The men grew worried. "Don't give up hope," Sir Ernest told them. "Remember, our ice floe is drifting. Every day we float closer to Elephant Island."

Elephant Island was nothing but a large rock. To Shackleton's men, however, it was the only hope. If they drifted past it, they would surely die. Past the island lay 3,000 miles of open ocean.

By April 8, 1916, the ice was splitting up. Sharp pieces of ice filled the water. Shackleton didn't want to launch the lifeboats. He feared the ice would tear the boats. But that night their ice floe cracked into two

Shackelton and his men wait to begin their journey.

pieces. The men just had time to jump onto one half before the other half drifted out of reach.

The next day, Sir Ernest gathered the men. "Launch the boats," he said.

The Journey To Elephant Island

In the lifeboats, the men had new problems. As they rowed into open water, the wind grew stronger. Waves 30 feet high sprayed freezing water into the boats. **Frostbite** began to set in. Hunger and thirst also weakened them. One man noted in his diary, "No sleep for 48 hours. All wet and cold with a blizzard **raging**."

For five days and nights, they sat in the three small boats. The salt water gave them bleeding sores all over their bodies. Their arms ached from rowing. Their toes ached from the cold.

Sir Ernest suffered as much as anyone, but he never let it show. He stood at the front of one boat, searching for Elephant Island. The wind cut into him. The water soaked him. Still, he stayed at his post.

"He is a wonderful man," wrote one man. "He simply never spares himself if, by his **toil**, he can possibly help anyone else."

At last Elephant Island appeared in the distance. "Most of us hardly knew whether to laugh or cry," wrote one man.

Like the others, Shackleton was happy to be on dry land. But he knew he could not stay there. The island could not support life. No ship ever came to Elephant Island, so there was no hope of being found.

"I am going to try to sail across the ocean to South Georgia," he told his crew. "I need five men to come with me."

Shackleton chose five of the men who offered to come. None of these men wanted to climb into a boat again. But they knew it was their only hope.

Across Cape Horn

On April 24, the six men rowed away from Elephant Island. They had to cross 800 miles of open ocean in a 22-foot boat. This stretch of ocean, called Cape Horn, is the stormiest in the world. The men who stayed behind feared the boat wouldn't make it. They feared they would die on Elephant Island.

In open waters, the boat moved swiftly. But it was an awful trip. Every minute and a half the boat was lifted onto 50-foot waves. As it crashed back down into the water, the men held on to the sides so they wouldn't be washed overboard. Hour after hour they struggled against the waves. Winds roared at them at 80 miles per hour. Their drinking water ran out. Their tongues became **swollen** from **thirst**.

After two weeks, they neared the island of South Georgia. They searched for seaweed or a stick of wood or some other sign of land. They knew that if they were off course, they would die. The waves would carry them out to the middle of the Atlantic. At last, on May 8, they caught sight of South Georgia.

Even after they landed, their journey was not over. All the people lived on the other side of the island. "We cannot sail around to the other side," said Sir Ernest. "Our boat is too badly battered. We will have to cross South Georgia on foot."

Shackleton left the three weakest men on the shore. He and the two others set out to walk the 29 miles to the town of Stromness. They clawed their way up mountains 4,500 feet high. They stumbled along frozen rocks and slid down steep cliffs. At last, on May 20, they reached Stromness. They were weak, frostbitten, and dangerously thin. But they were alive.

Quickly a ship was sent to get the three men on the other side of South Georgia. They were picked up easily. But bad weather kept ships from getting to Elephant Island. At last, on August 30, 1916, Shackleton landed a ship there. To his joy, he found all 22 men still alive. The group had seen amazingly rough times. But every single man came out alive.

Do You Remember?

■ In the blank, write the letter of the best ending for each sentence.

_____ 1. Shackleton was trying to
   a. cross Antarctica.
   b. find the source of the Niger.
   c. circle the globe.

_____ 2. Elephant Island was
   a. nothing but a large rock.   b. hot.   c. covered with trees.

_____ 3. Shackleton left Elephant Island because
   a. his men no longer trusted him.
   b. he was dying.
   c. he wanted to get help for his men.

_____ 4. Shackleton and five other men crossed Cape Horn
   a. on an ice floe.   b. in a small boat.   c. on foot.

_____ 5. When Shackleton returned to Elephant Island,
   a. everyone had disappeared.
   b. all 22 men were dead.
   c. all 22 men were still alive.

Express Yourself

■ Pretend you are one of Shackleton's men. Sir Ernest is about to set off for South Georgia. You are staying behind on Elephant Island. Write a journal entry describing your feelings.

_____

_____

_____

_____

_____

Exploring Words

■ Read each sentence. Fill in the circle next to the best meaning for the word in dark print. If you need help, use the Glossary.

1. The **slabs** of ice began to break up.
   ○ a. thick, flat pieces   ○ b. small sleds   ○ c. wide rivers

2. The men broke through a **layer** of ice.
   ○ a. hidden cave   ○ b. sheet   ○ c. pool

3. Shackleton decided to **launch** the boats.
   ○ a. put into the water   ○ b. get rid of   ○ c. clean

4. Most of the men had **frostbite**.
   ○ a. warm winter clothing
   ○ b. trouble breathing
   ○ c. frozen body parts

5. The **floes** floated out toward the open sea.
   ○ a. sheets of ice   ○ b. Antarctic plants   ○ c. boats

6. The men struggled through a **raging** storm.
   ○ a. winter   ○ b. ocean   ○ c. very strong

7. The men's tongues became **swollen**.
   ○ a. red   ○ b. larger than usual   ○ c. sore

8. The ice was no longer **solid**.
   ○ a. hard   ○ b. dirty   ○ c. cold

9. **Thirst** became a problem for the men.
   ○ a. the need for water
   ○ b. the need for sleep
   ○ c. the weather

10. Shackleton always helped others by his **toil**.
    ○ a. quick mind   ○ b. kindness   ○ c. hard work

Margaret Mead

Margaret Mead leaned out the train window.

"Good-bye! Good-bye!" she called to her family as the train pulled out of the station.

Margaret's eyes danced with excitement. She was on her way! Soon she would be on a ship sailing to the South Seas. She planned to spend the whole year of 1925 in Samoa, studying Samoan **customs**. At 23, Margaret had never been out of the United States before. She had never stayed alone in a hotel. In fact, she later wrote, "I had never spent a day in my life alone."

A Lot to Learn

In Samoa, Margaret lived on a **remote** island called Tau. Margaret lived with the Holts, an American family. Mr. Holt was in the Navy. Margaret spent most of her time in the villages. She wanted to learn all she could about Samoan teenage girls.

Margaret faced many **challenges** in Samoa. She had to learn a new language. Samoan is a very difficult language to learn. Margaret spent many hours each day studying. After six weeks, she had learned to speak and understand Samoan.

Year Of Challenges

The weather in Samoa was also a challenge. The air was hot and wet. It rained five times every day. These were no ordinary showers. One visitor said the raindrops were the size of almonds. Between storms, the sun beat down with such strength that it made Margaret **dizzy**.

Margaret had trouble getting used to Samoan food. She was also bothered by flies. Millions of them flew around her head. When talking to the village girls, she had to sit in the correct Samoan **style**. That meant

sitting cross-legged for hours at a time. At the end of such talks, Margaret's legs were so stiff she could **barely** walk.

"After a few hours in a **native** house, one gets a sense of heavy, almost sticky heat," she wrote. "It feels as if one's skin were going to fly off in layers. One also gets a **curious** buzzing inside one's head."

Margaret learned to deal with all of this. She also had to deal with her own **loneliness**. She had no newspapers and no telephone. Every few weeks a boat brought letters from home. But beyond that, she was cut off from everything and everyone she knew.

Hurricane!

Margaret spent Christmas Day 1925 with the Holts and their two small children. She was with them on New Year's Day, too. On that day a hurricane blasted the tiny island of Tau. Rain poured down, and wind whipped through the streets. The storm destroyed the

schools. Even the hospital caved in. "It was pouring rain and the air was full of flying sand, coconuts, parts of tin roofs, and so on," Margaret later wrote. The wind ripped the porch and the front doors off the Holts' house.

Two men managed to break open the water tank that stood outside the Holts' home. After the water rushed out, Mr. Holt told Margaret to climb in. He handed her the baby. Then the rest of the family squeezed in. They stayed there until the storm ended. When they crawled out, the island was a wreck. Only a few churches and the Holts' home were still standing.

Despite everything, Margaret never gave up. She finished her work in Samoa. In 1928, she wrote a book about it. The book was called Coming of Age in Samoa. It became a best seller. For Margaret, though, it was only a beginning. Over the next 50 years, she studied many other peoples and wrote 40 other books. Her work changed the way we look at ourselves and our world.

Do You Remember?

■ Read each sentence below. Write **T** if the sentence is true. Write **F** if the sentence is false.

_____ 1. Margaret never learned the Samoan language.

_____ 2. Margaret lived with the Holt family.

_____ 3. It almost never rained in Samoa.

_____ 4. Margaret Mead never felt lonely in Samoa.

_____ 5. On January 1, 1926, a hurricane hit the island of Tau.

_____ 6. The hurricane completely destroyed the Holts' home.

_____ 7. Margaret wrote a book about her time in Samoa.

_____ 8. Margaret studied many other peoples.

Critical Thinking — Drawing Conclusions

■ Complete the following sentences.

1. Margaret went to Samoa because _____

_____

2. Margaret's legs became stiff when talking to the village girls because

_____

3. Margaret and the Holts climbed into the empty water tank because

_____

4. Margaret felt lonely because _____

_____

5. The weather in Samoa was a challenge because _____

_____

Exploring Words

■ Use the words in the box to complete the paragraphs. Reread the paragraphs to be sure they make sense.

curious	dizzy	style	loneliness	challenges
Despite	native	barely	remote	customs

Margaret Mead spent a year in Samoa studying Samoan

(1) _____ . Margaret faced many (2) _____ during this

year. She lived on the (3) _____ island of Tau. She had little

contact with the outside world. Because of this, she felt great

(4) _____ .

Margaret faced other problems, too. The sun made her

(5) _____ . She had trouble sitting in the correct Samoan

(6) _____ . Her legs got so stiff she could (7) _____

walk. She felt a (8) _____ buzzing in her head whenever she

spent much time in a (9) _____ house. (10) _____

these difficulties, Margaret did not give up.

The Kon-Tiki

Thor Heyerdahl had made up his mind. He and five other men would sail 4,300 miles from South America to the South Sea Islands. And they would do it on a **raft**. Most sailors laughed at Heyerdahl. "Rafts are not for sailing," they told him. "They go sideways and **backwards** and round as the wind takes them."

Heyerdahl's friends begged him not to go. One talked about what might happen to Heyerdahl's wife and children. Another said, "Your mother and father will be very sad when they hear of your **death**."

Heyerdahl's Idea

Still, Heyerdahl stuck to his plans. He wanted to test his idea about South Sea Islanders. Heyerdahl's idea was simple. He believed the first Islanders came from the South American country of Peru.

Scientists laughed at this idea. They said that South America was too far away. Besides, the people of **ancient** Peru had no ships. Heyerdahl knew this. He said the Peruvians didn't sail on ships. They floated across the Pacific on rafts!

In 1947, most people could not accept this idea. So Heyerdahl decided to make his own raft to sail across the ocean. He would use the same tools that the people of ancient Peru used. If he made it to the South Sea Islands, people would have to listen to him. Heyerdahl made his raft out of **balsa** wood logs. He named it Kon-Tiki after a Peruvian god. The raft was 40 feet long and 18 feet wide. There was no metal in it. After all, ancient Peruvians had no metal. Heyerdahl tied all the logs together with rope. The Kon-Tiki had a bamboo deck and cabin. It also had a simple square sail and a 19-foot-long steering oar.

Staying Afloat

On the morning of April 29, 1947, Heyerdahl and his crew set out. They did not know whether they would ever see land again. They had to trust the winds and the ocean **currents**. With luck, Heyerdahl thought, they would reach the South Sea Islands in about three months.

Could the Kon-Tiki stay above water that long? One expert told Heyerdahl that the logs would soak up water. "Your raft will sink before you have covered a quarter of the distance across the sea," he said.

A boat maker said that the ropes would never hold

ASIA

Pacific Ocean

NORTH AMERICA

South Sea Islands

Lima

SOUTH AMERICA

Heyerdahl studies a shark aboard the Kon-Tiki.

the wood together. "The logs will bounce around in the waves. In a few weeks they will wear through all the ropes, and the raft will fall apart," he warned.

Heyerdahl worried about these **warnings**. After all, he had never sailed a balsa wood raft before. Maybe it would sink! After a few days at sea, he saw that the logs did soak up water. When no one was looking, he poked his finger into a log. Water bubbled out. Heyerdahl then tore off a piece of the log. He dropped it into the sea and sadly watched it sink.

But the Kon-Tiki did not sink. Heyerdahl's crew had cut down fresh balsa trees. The **sap** inside the green logs sealed out the water. Only the outer inch got wet. This wet layer helped the raft. The ropes wore their way into the wet part of the wood. This protected the ropes when the logs rubbed together.

Weeks passed. The Kon-Tiki, bouncing up and down like a cork, floated west. The water currents carried it straight toward the South Seas. On July 4, a bad storm struck. The raft twisted and turned in the rough sea. Some waves towered 25 feet above the raft. The men held tightly to the ropes as water rushed across the deck. Everyone was afraid of getting washed overboard because the raft could not be turned around. Luckily, everyone made it. The tough little raft proved it could weather the worst ocean storms.

Man Overboard!

A few days later, however, something awful happened. A sleeping bag fell over the side of the raft. Herman Watzinger saw it. As he reached for it, he tripped and fell into the water. Heyerdahl heard Watzinger's cry. He saw his friend splashing wildly in the water. "Man overboard!" he yelled.

Watzinger was a fine swimmer. But he had no chance of catching up to the raft in the rough sea. The men tossed a life belt to him. The belt was tied to the raft by a long rope. But the strong wind just blew the belt back in their faces. For a moment, it seemed that Watzinger was lost forever.

Then, suddenly, Knut Haugland grabbed the life belt. He dove into the water. Haugland and Watzinger swam **desperately** towards each other. At last they touched hands. Haugland waved to the Kon-Tiki. The four men on the raft pulled him and Watzinger back to safety.

At last, on the morning of July 30, Watzinger spotted land. It was a tiny island named Puka Puka. The raft had passed it during the night. The men tried to change course. But the current carried them away from the island. On August 3, they tried to land at another island. But the wind made it impossible.

On August 6, they spotted the dangerous Raroia **coral reef**. Waves crashed angrily against the sharp rocks. They didn't want to land here! But they had no choice. As the Kon-Tiki drifted toward shore, the men got ready for the worst.

Heyerdahl made one final note in his book. "Very close now. Drifting along the reef. Only a hundred yards or so away. Must pack up the log now. All in good spirits; it looks bad, but we shall make it!"

As the Kon-Tiki drifted closer, huge waves crashed across its decks. The raft bounced madly up and down. Heyerdahl shouted to his men, "Hold on! Never mind about the cargo. Hold on!"

One huge wave after another battered the men and the raft. Then the biggest wave of all hit. It smashed the raft like a toy against the reef. The Kon-Tiki was now nothing but a tangle of twisted logs. Yet somehow the men managed to hang onto it. Finally the raft reached the rocks. The men climbed off the raft and made their way to the shore.

Thor Heyerdahl had made it. He had proven that it was possible to float across the Pacific on a raft. His trip forced scientists to think differently. People saw that Thor Heyerdahl wasn't crazy after all.

Do You Remember?

■ In the blank, write the letter of the best ending for each sentence.

_____ 1. Heyerdahl believed that the first South Sea Islanders came from

a. Europe.   b. South America.   c. Africa.

_____ 2. Heyerdahl and his crew made their raft out of

a. balsa wood.   b. coral.   c. metal.

_____ 3. Kon-Tiki was the name of

a. Heyerdahl's wife.

b. a Peruvian god.

c. an island in the South Seas.

_____ 4. A boat maker told Heyerdahl that his raft would

a. be hit by lightning.

b. be eaten by sharks.

c. fall apart.

_____ 5. Herman Watzinger almost died when

a. he fell overboard.

b. Knut Haugland hit him.

c. he became ill.

Express Yourself

■ Pretend you are Thor Heyerdahl's son or daughter. Your father is getting ready to sail the Kon-Tiki across the Pacific. What would you want to say to him before he left?

_____

_____

_____

_____

_____

Exploring Words

■ Use the clues to complete the puzzle. Choose from the words in the box.

raft

backwards

death

coral reef

ancient

balsa

currents

sap

warnings

desperately

Across

3. very old
7. a flat, square kind of boat
8. being told about danger
9. wildly
10. the juice inside plants

Down

1. with the back part in front
2. the end of life
4. a thin wall of stony material
5. a strong, light kind of wood.
6. water that moves a certain direction

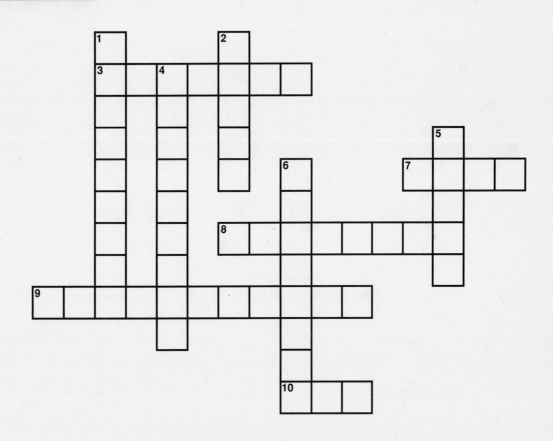

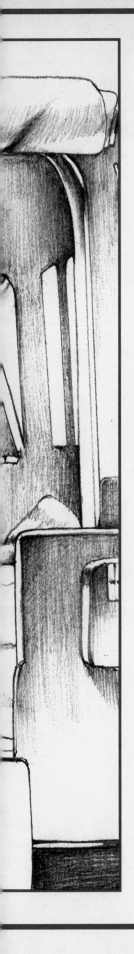

Joy Adamson

"**J**oy, where are you? Quick, I have something for you."

Joy Adamson hurried out of her tent in northern Kenya, a country in Africa. She ran over to the car where her husband, George, was waiting for her.

"What is it?" she asked.

George pointed to the back of the car. There lay three tiny lion cubs. They were hiding their faces between their paws in fear. Joy's heart filled with love when she saw them. Carefully she reached out and touched one. Then she scooped all three into her arms.

Raising Three Cubs

"The mother attacked me," George told Joy sadly. As a **game warden**, he often faced angry wild animals. "She was coming right at me. I didn't have a choice. I had to shoot her. But I brought the babies home with me. I couldn't leave them to die."

Joy nodded. She also couldn't bear the thought of letting these babies die. "They were only a few days old," she later wrote. "Their eyes were still covered with a **bluish film**. They could hardly crawl. How could I **resist** them?"

Joy made a bed for the cubs in her tent. She fed them milk from a bottle. She played games with them and took them for walks. After a few days, the cubs had become part of the family. Each one had its own **personality**. Big One was the largest and quietest of the three. Lustica loved to clown around. And Elsa, the littlest and the weakest, was the most curious.

For five months the three lion cubs scampered around the Adamson's home. But, by July 1956, Joy knew something had to be done. The cubs were growing bigger every day. Their teeth and claws were becoming dangerously sharp. The young lions were also getting very strong. They were always gentle with the Adamsons. But Joy knew the growing lions couldn't stay there forever. Sadly, she and George sent two of them off to a zoo in Holland. Elsa was still the weakest. Joy decided to keep her until she was fully grown.

Elsa Grows Up

At first, Elsa missed her sisters. But she soon learned to play by herself. Joy and George set up a little playground for her. They hung a tire swing from a tree. They gave her a wooden barrel to roll around in. And they gave her old sheets to chew on.

Elsa loved her life with the Adamsons. When Joy or George went for a ride, Elsa went, too. She lay on the roof of the truck as it bounced along. Once Joy and George took a vacation. They went to the Indian Ocean. Elsa went with them. She splashed happily in the salt water.

Back home, Joy often took Elsa out into the bush. Elsa learned to chase zebras, giraffes, and buffalo. Most lions kill these animals for food. But Elsa didn't know how to kill. She had no mother to teach her.

Sometimes Elsa cornered an animal. But at the last minute, she always became scared. Then she backed away and let the animal escape.

Elsa wasn't worried about finding food. She knew that Joy would feed her. Elsa had complete trust in Joy. She trusted Joy to feed her and keep her safe. She often climbed into Joy's bed. She even let Joy pull out a tooth that was loose.

Joy loved Elsa's gentle ways. But she knew that soon even gentle Elsa would have to go to a zoo. Elsa was 23 months old. She was almost fully grown.

With great sadness, Joy started to think about zoos. Elsa, however, had other ideas. In January, 1958, she suddenly ran off into the bush.

"**Normally** Elsa followed us on our walks wherever we went," wrote Joy. "But on this afternoon, she led us in her direction. We soon found the fresh marks of a lion. At dark, she refused to return. We called desperately for Elsa. No **familiar** sound came in answer. But **presently** we heard a **chorus** of lions a few hundred yards away."

After five hours, Elsa finally came back. She was tired and thirsty. Joy and George knew she had been out running with wild lions.

Suddenly, Joy was not sure Elsa belonged in a zoo. Perhaps she could be returned to the wild. No other tame lion had ever learned to live free. Tame lions did not know how to hunt. They carried a human scent which made other lions stay away from them. But perhaps Elsa was different. Perhaps she was smart enough to learn hunting skills. And perhaps she could win the trust of wild lions. With a mixture of hope and fear, the Adamsons decided to set Elsa free.

Finding Freedom

First, the Adamsons had to teach Elsa how to kill. George shot a small animal and took it to her. He let her eat it. In this way, she learned that dead animals could serve as food. The Adamsons also took Elsa to a spot where wild lions had killed a zebra. By watching them, Elsa learned how other lions ate.

At last the Adamsons decided to give Elsa a test. They drove her far from camp and set her free. After a few days they returned. Poor Elsa was very glad to see them. Clearly she didn't understand why they had gone away. And clearly she had eaten nothing since they left.

George tried to teach Elsa more about killing. He took her hunting. When she cornered an animal, he shot it for her. Then he let her eat it. Slowly Elsa learned how to kill for herself.

Elsa also learned how to make friends with other lions. When Joy and George set her free, she often ran off with lions. But after two or three days, she always came back.

For a year, the Adamsons worked at setting Elsa free. Finally, in February 1959, she was ready. One day a handsome male lion called to her. Elsa went charging off with him. Wrote Joy, "It was **obvious** that she was in love." Over the next few days, she made a few trips back to the Adamson's camp. But she never stayed long. And when she did come, her stomach was full. Joy and George were thrilled. Elsa was killing her own food! And she had found a mate. It was hard for Joy to say goodbye to Elsa. But she knew that Elsa was happy and healthy. And most importantly, Elsa was where she belonged, living free with other lions.

Do You Remember?

■ In the blank, write the letter of the best ending for each sentence.

_____ 1. Elsa's mother was killed by
        a. hunters.   b. wild elephants.   c. George.

_____ 2. Of the three cubs, Elsa was the
        a. quietest.   b. most curious.   c. largest.

_____ 3. When Elsa went to the Indian Ocean, she
        a. played happily in the water.
        b. attacked Joy.
        c. ran off with wild lions.

_____ 4. George taught Elsa how to
        a. kill for food.   b. run.   c. live in a cage.

_____ 5. Elsa finally found
        a. her mother and father.   b. her sisters.   c. a mate.

Critical Thinking – Finding the Sequence

■ Number the sentences to show the order in which things happened in the story. The first one is done for you.

_____ Joy fed Elsa milk from a bottle.

_____ The Adamsons set Elsa free.

__1__ George brought home three lion cubs.

_____ Elsa went running with wild lions for the first time.

_____ Big One and Lustica were sent to a zoo.

Exploring Words

■ Write the correct word in each sentence.

resist	personality	familiar	presently	chorus
bluish	game warden	obvious	normally	film

1. A person whose job it is to make sure people don't break hunting and fishing laws is a _____.

2. When something looks somewhat blue it is called _____.

3. A group of people or animals speaking or crying out at the same time is a _____.

4. When something usually happens, it _____ happens.

5. A thin covering is a _____.

6. When you have heard something many times before and know it well, that sound is _____ to you.

7. Something that will happen soon will happen _____.

8. Something that is very clear to you is _____.

9. The things that make you different from others make up your _____.

10. When you try to keep from enjoying or liking something, you _____ it.

To the Top of Annapurna

Arlene Blum spoke softly into her **tape recorder**. "There were so many **avalanches** yesterday," she said. "It gives you a scary feeling. I keep wondering when the next avalanche will come."

Blum stopped for a moment. She glanced up at the snow-covered mountain named Annapurna. Would the snow come rushing down again today? And if it did, would it sweep her and the others away? Blum felt fear in the pit of her stomach. She spoke into the tape recorder once more. "Maybe we shouldn't climb today," she said.

The whole team is ready to begin the climb.

Taking On Annapurna

Blum and her crew did end up climbing on that day. After all, that was why they had come to this 26,504 foot mountain in Nepal, a country north of India. They wanted to climb Annapurna. It was the tenth highest mountain in the world. Few people had ever reached its **summit**. Seven had died trying.

Arlene Blum's team was the first of its kind. Its members were all women. No all-woman group had ever climbed a mountain this high. Blum's group used Sherpa guides who were men, just as other climbing teams did. But everyone else was a woman.

The women began climbing on August 28, 1978. They soon hit ice walls 500 feet high. The **threat** of a **deadly** avalanche always hung over them. They ran into wild storms. During one blizzard, their Sherpa guides quit. But Blum promised them more money. They agreed to come back.

Finally, on October 13, the team reached the 24,200-foot mark. There they set up a camp. Two days later, they would make the final push for the top.

On Top

Blum picked two small groups to climb to the summit. The rest would stay at the camp. For the first group Blum chose Piro Kramer, Irene Miller, and Vera Komarkova. She picked two Sherpa guides to go with them.

The group woke up at 3 A.M. on October 15. It was about ten **degrees** below zero. That far up, there was not much **oxygen** in the air. Everyone had to move slowly. While she was getting ready, Kramer took off her gloves. The tip of one finger was frozen. She knew right away that she would not go to the top. She said, "I'd rather lose the summit than my finger."

At 7 A.M. the others began the final climb. The snow was sometimes up to their knees. They had to breathe six times just to take one step. Often they wondered if they could keep going. But none of them quit. They just kept climbing. At last, at 3:30 P.M., all four reached the top. The women stuck an American flag into the snow. Then they hugged each other. They had made it!

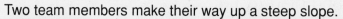

Two team members make their way up a steep slope.

A Sad Ending

A second team tried to reach the summit two days later. Their guide soon got sick. He returned to the camp. But Vera Watson and Alison Chadwick kept going. That night Blum tried to reach the two women by radio. She got no answer. In the morning she scanned the mountain. She could not see Watson or Chadwick. Fear grew with each passing minute. What had happened to them?

Two days later that question was answered. Guides had been sent to look for the two women. They spotted the bodies of Watson and Chadwick lying at the bottom of a 1,500 foot cliff. One of them had probably slipped on the ice. Since they were roped together, they had both fallen to their death. The team's joy instantly turned to sadness.

Carefully the team went back down the mountain. They had completed the toughest climb of their lives. They had conquered Annapurna. But they had also lost two dear friends. For Blum and the others, Annapurna would always be a **symbol** of both **victory** and **loss**.

Do You Remember?

■ Read each sentence below. Write **T** if the sentence is true. Write **F** if the sentence is false.

_____ 1. The only men in Blum's group were the Sherpa guides.

_____ 2. Annapurna is the highest mountain in the world.

_____ 3. Blum's team faced blizzards and avalanches.

_____ 4. Piro Kramer did not go to the top because her finger was frozen.

_____ 5. The first group Blum picked gave up before they made it to the top.

_____ 6. An American flag was stuck into the snow on top of Annapurna.

_____ 7. Arlene Blum died trying to climb Annapurna.

_____ 8. Watson and Chadwick were killed by Sherpa guides.

Express Yourself

■ Pretend you are a member of Arlene Blum's team. Write an entry in your journal explaining why you have decided to climb Annapurna.

_____

_____

_____

_____

_____

_____

Exploring Words

■ Read each sentence. Fill in the circle next to the best meaning for the word in dark print. If you need help, use the Glossary.

1. Arlene Blum brought a **tape recorder** with her.
   - ○ a. tool used to measure distance
   - ○ b. a machine that can record and play back sounds
   - ○ c. first aid supplies

2. The group saw several **avalanches**.
   - ○ a. wild animals   ○ b. unfriendly climbers   ○ c. snow slides

3. The first group reached the **summit** safely.
   - ○ a. lowest part   ○ b. highest part   ○ c. tent

4. It was ten **degrees** below zero.
   - ○ a. measure of temperature
   - ○ b. measure of distance
   - ○ c. minutes

5. There was the **threat** of another storm.
   - ○ a. sound   ○ b. danger   ○ c. hope

6. For two women, the climb was **deadly**.
   - ○ a. able to kill   ○ b. easy   ○ c. not exciting

7. There was not much **oxygen** at that height.
   - ○ a. noise   ○ b. light   ○ c. gas in the air

8. The flag was an important **symbol**.
   - ○ a. joke
   - ○ b. piece of cloth
   - ○ c. something that stands for something else

9. Getting to the top was a great **victory**.
   - ○ a. climb   ○ b. something that makes you sad   ○ c. success

10. The women were saddened by the **loss** of their friends.
    - ○ a. angry words   ○ b. act of losing   ○ c. strange actions

Glossary

advanced, page 5
To be advanced is to be ahead of others.

advisers, page 7
Your advisers are people who help you decide what to do.

ancient, page 66
Ancient means very old.

assignment, page 32
An assignment is a job you are given to do.

avalanches, page 80
An avalanche is the fall of a great deal of snow and ice down the side of a mountain.

backwards, page 65
Backwards means with the back part in front.

bailed, page 13
If you bailed out a boat, you used a bucket to empty water out of it.

balsa, page 66
The balsa tree is a kind of tree with strong, light wood.

bandit, page 3
A bandit is a thief.

barely, page 60
Barely means hardly.

blank, page 19
Blank means empty or without writing.

bloody, page 27
Bloody means covered with blood, or causing harm to many people.

bluish, page 74
Bluish means somewhat blue.

boasted, page 34
If you boasted, you spoke with too much pride about something.

cannibals, page 38
Cannibals are people who eat the bodies of dead humans.

carrier pigeon, page 46
A carrier pigeon is a bird that has been taught to carry messages.

challenges, page 59
Challenges are things one has to work very hard to do.

chorus, page 76
A chorus is a group of people or animals all speaking or crying out at the same time.

civilized, page 34
Civilized countries are highly developed.

clams, page 15
Clams are shellfish.

collapsed, page 22
If you collapsed, you reached the end of your strength.

compass, page 21

A compass is an instrument for showing direction, with a needle that always points north.

continent, page 29

A continent is a large piece of land with water all around it.

convince, page 41

To convince someone of something is to make them believe that it is true.

coral reef, page 69

A coral reef is a thin line of stony material. Coral reefs are found near the surface of the water.

cramped, page 14

If your muscles cramped, they became painfully tight.

curious, page 60

To be curious is to want to learn about things.

currents, page 66

A current is water in an ocean or river that moves in a certain direction.

customs, page 58

Customs are the things that are usually done by a group of people.

deadly, page 81

Something that is deadly is able to kill.

death, page 65

Death is the end of life.

degrees, page 82

A degree is a measure of temperature.

desperately, page 68

When you do something desperately, you do it wildly.

despite, page 61

Despite means in spite of.

diary, page 21

A diary is a book where people write down what happens to them every day.

disease, page 26

To have a disease is to be sick.

dizzy, page 59

When you feel dizzy, you feel as though everything around you were moving.

editor, page 32

An editor is a person who corrects pieces of writing and gets them ready to print.

engineers, page 5

An engineer is a person who makes plans for building things.

equipment, page 45

Equipment means things that have a special use.

excellent, page 46

Excellent means very good.

exhausted, page 13

Exhausted means very tired.

failure, page 35

To be a failure means not to be able to do what you had set out to do.

familiar, page 76
If something is familiar to you, you know it well.

fantastic, page 6
Something that is fantastic is very strange.

fate, page 47
A person's fate is what happens to her or him.

film, page 74
A film is a thin covering.

floes, page 52
Floes are sheets of ice floating on water.

frostbite, page 53
Frostbite is when part of a person's body freezes.

game warden, page 74
A game warden is a person whose job it is to make sure people don't break hunting and fishing laws.

glorious, page 46
Glorious means wonderful.

gracefully, page 46
Gracefully means in a smooth and easy way.

hostile, page 26
Hostile means unfriendly.

illness, page 47
Illness means being sick.

imaginary, page 33
Something imaginary is made up and not real.

informed, page 34
If you kept someone informed, you let him or her know what was happening.

inspired, page 7
If something inspired you, it made you want to do something.

ivory, page 39
Ivory is a material made from the tusks of elephants or other animals.

launch, page 52
To launch a boat is to put it into the water.

layer, page 51
A layer is a sheet of something.

leeches, page 41
Leeches are worms that live in water and drink animals' blood.

loneliness, page 60
Loneliness is the feeling of being alone.

loss, page 83
Loss is the act of losing something.

majestic, page 22
Something majestic is very grand.

mightiest, page 29
Mightiest means largest or strongest.

mission, page 22
A mission is what a person is sent to do.

Moslems, page 21

Moslems are people who believe in Islam.

mutiny, page 12

A mutiny is when soldiers or sailors rise up against the people in charge of them.

native, page 60

Native means of or belonging to the people who were born in a place.

nightmare, page 28

A nightmare is a bad dream, or something that happens in real life that seems like a bad dream.

normally, page 76

Normally means usually.

obvious, page 77

Obvious means clear to see.

odor, page 47

Something's odor is its smell.

opportunity, page 41

An opportunity is a chance.

ounce, page 12

An ounce is a measure of weight. There are 16 ounces in a pound.

overboard, page 34

Overboard means off a ship or boat.

oxygen, page 82

Oxygen is one of the gases in air that people need to live.

paces, page 6

A pace is the distance a person can cover with one step.

personality, page 74

A person's or animal's personality is what makes him, her, or it different from others.

pierced, page 29

To pierce means to go all the way through.

poisonous, page 40

Poisonous means able to kill or cause harm with poison.

presently, page 76

Presently means soon.

punishment, page 12

Punishment is something bad done to someone who has broken a rule or done something wrong.

raft, page 65

A raft is a flat, square kind of boat.

raging, page 53

When someone says that a storm is raging, he or she means that the storm is very strong.

rapids, page 28

Rapids are a part of a river where the water flows very fast over and around rocks.

ration, page 12

To ration is to give out in equal shares.

remote, page 59

Remote means far away.

reporter, page 33

A reporter is someone who gathers news for a newspaper, magazine, radio, or T.V.

resist, page 74

To resist something means to keep from enjoying or liking it.

rot, page 13

To rot is to spoil or go bad.

sap, page 67

Sap is the juice inside plants.

savages, page 41

Savages are people whose way of life is rough and wild.

seams, page 45

Seams are the places where two pieces of cloth are sewn together.

seasick, page 33

To be seasick is to be made sick by the way a ship or boat moves in the water.

serpents, page 6

Serpents are snakes or snake–like animals.

shocked, page 41

To be shocked is to be surprised by something that is not pleasant.

sire, page 5

A king is called Sire.

slabs, page 51

A slab is a flat, thick piece of something.

solid, page 52

Something solid is hard.

source, page 28

The source of something is the place it comes from.

spat, page 21

If you spat, you forced water out of your mouth.

squinted, page 3

To squint is to look with the eyes closed part of the way.

struggled, page 13

If you struggled, you worked very hard.

style, page 59

A style is a certain way of doing something.

sucking, page 22

If you are sucking something, you are pulling liquid or juice from it with your mouth.

summit, page 81

The summit of something is its highest part.

survive, page 40

To survive something is to live through it.

swollen, page 55
Something that is swollen has become larger than usual.

symbol, page 83
A symbol is something that stands for something else.

tape recorder, page 80
A tape recorder is a machine that can record and play back sounds.

thirst, page 55
Thirst is the need for water.

threat, page 81
A threat is a danger.

toil, page 54
Toil is hard work.

traced, page 29
To trace something is to follow its course.

varnish, page 45
Varnish is a type of paint that forms a hard, clear surface.

victory, page 83
Victory is success.

volunteered, page 20
If you volunteered, you offered to do something.

waded, page 41
If you waded, you walked through water.

warnings, page 67
If someone gives you warnings, that person tells you about danger.

Chart Your Progress

Stories	Do You Remember?	Exploring Words	Critical Thinking	Express Yourself	Score
Marco Polo					/25
Amazing Voyage					/23
Search for the Niger					/19
Henry Morton Stanley					/23
Around the World					/26
Mary Kingsley					/20
Flight of the Eagle					/23
Sir Ernest Shackleton					/20
Margaret Mead					/23
The Kon-Tiki					/20
Joy Adamson					/20
To the Top of Annpurna					/23

Finding Your Score
1. Count the number of correct answers you have for each activity.
2. Write these numbers in the boxes in the chart.
3. Ask your teacher to give you a score (maximum score 5) for **Express Yourself**.
4. Add up the numbers to get a final score.

Answer Key

Marco Polo
Pages 2-9

Do You Remember? 1-c, 2-b, 3-b, 4-a, 5-c

Critical Thinking — Fact or Opinion? 1-O, 2-F, 3-F, 4-O, 5-F, 6-O, 7-F, 8-F, 9-O, 10-F

Exploring Words: 1. fantastic, 2. paces, 3. Sire, 4. bandit, 5. advanced, 6. engineers, 7. serpents, 8. inspired, 9. advisers, 10. squinted

Amazing Voyage
Pages 10-17

Do You Remember? 1-F, 2-F, 3-T, 4-F, 5-T, 6-F, 7-T, 8-T

Express Yourself: Answers will vary.

Exploring Words: 1-c, 2-b, 3-b, 4-a, 5-b, 6-c, 7-a, 8-a, 9-a, 10-b

Search for the Niger
Pages 18-25

Do You Remember? 1-b, 2-c, 3-b, 4-b, 5-a

Critical Thinking — Drawing Conclusions:
Answers will vary.
Here are some examples.
1. he was eager for adventure.
2. he knew Ali was planning to kill him.
3. he and his horse collapsed.
4. he got tired of waiting for volunteers.

Exploring Words:

1. volunteered 2. blank, 3. compass, 4. diary, 5. mission, 6. Moslems, 7. spat, 8. sucking, 9. majestic, 10. collapsed

Henry Morton Stanley
Pages 26-31

Do You Remember? 1-T, 2-F, 3-T, 4-F, 5-T, 6-F, 7-F, 8-T

Express Yourself: Answers will vary.

Exploring Words: Across: 2. bloody, 5. mightiest, 7. continent, 8. rapids, 10. disease
Down: 1. hostile, 3. pierced, 4. nightmare, 6. traced, 9. source

Around the World
Pages 32-37

Do You Remember? 1-F, 2-T, 3-F, 4-T, 5-F, 6-T, 7-T, 8-F

Critical Thinking–Fact or Opinion? 1-O, 2-F, 3-O, 4-F, 5-F, 6-O, 7-F, 8-O

Exploring Words: 1. reporter, 2. editor, 3. assignment, 4. boasted, 5. imaginary, 6. seasick, 7. overboard, 8. informed, 9. civilized, 10. failure

Mary Kingsley
Pages 38-43

Do You Remember? 1-a, 2-b, 3-a, 4-b, 5-c

Express Yourself: Answers will vary.

Exploring Words: 1. survive, 2. poisonous, 3. opportunity, 4. cannibals, 5. shocked, 6. leeches, 7. convince, 8. savages, 9. waded, 10. ivory

Flight of the Eagle
Pages 44-49

Do You Remember? 1-T, 2-F, 3-T, 4-F, 5-T, 6-F, 7-T, 8-F

Critical Thinking–Main Ideas: 2, 4

Exploring Words: Across: 1. glorious,

5. carrier pigeon, 7. illness,
9. varnish, 10. fate
Down: 2. odor, 3. excellent,
4. gracefully, 6. equipment, 8. seams

Sir Ernest Shackleton

Pages 50-57

Do You Remember? 1-a, 2-a, 3-c,
4-b 5-c

Express Yourself: Answers will vary.

Exploring Words: 1-a, 2-b, 3-a, 4-c,
5-a, 6-c, 7-b, 8-a, 9-a, 10-c

Margaret Mead

Pages 58-63

Do You Remember? 1-F, 2-T,
3-F, 4-F, 5-T, 6-F, 7-T, 8-T

Critical Thinking — Cause and Effect:
Answers will vary.
Here are some examples.
1. she wanted to study Samoan
   customs.
2. she had to sit cross-legged for
   hours at a time.
3. they wanted to find safety during
   the hurricane.
4. she had no telephone,
   newspapers, or outside visitors.
5. it was very hot and it rained
   five times a day.

Exploring Words: 1. customs,
2. challenges, 3. remote, 4. loneliness,
5. dizzy, 6. style, 7. barely,
8. curious, 9. native, 10. Despite

The Kon-Tiki

Pages 64-71

Do You Remember? 1-b, 2-a, 3-b,
4-c, 5-a

Express Yourself: Answers will vary.

Exploring Words: Across: 3. ancient,
7. raft, 8. warnings, 9. desperately,
10. sap
Down: 1. backwards, 2. death,
4. coral reef, 5. balsa, 6. currents

Joy Adamson

Pages 72-79

Do You Remember? 1-c,
2-b, 3-a, 4-a, 5-c

**Critical Thinking — Finding the
Sequence:** 2, 5, 1, 4, 3

Exploring Words: 1. game warden,
2. bluish, 3. chorus, 4. normally,
5. film, 6. familiar, 7. presently,
8. obvious, 9. personality, 10. resist

To the Top of Annapurna

Pages 80-85

Do You Remember? 1-T, 2-F, 3-T,
4-T, 5-F, 6-T, 7-F, 8-F

Express Yourself: Answers will vary.

Exploring Words: 1-b, 2-c, 3-b, 4-a,
5-b, 6-a, 7-c, 8-c, 9-c, 10-b